MMXXII

for
Frances
Charles
Graham
Ivy
& Yishai

# Contents

All the sky is a ship
And the constellations
Loves we cannot reach

# The Ballad of Shelby and Joel

I

Palace, one of a thousand
Garage for two cars
Princes! Striking handsome
View of the stars,
Rainbow you sister muses,
Seven dwarves!
Recruit me cold monsters
Frozen to the core.

II

Perfidy: echo of games
Telling me lies, am I insane?
Composing my love for your frame.
I'm beginning to be ashamed of this.

III

She's got the powers of metamorphosis:
Turn it all to gold with a curtsey or a kiss.
She's got the space she needs
To back out out of this, Iphigenia to them
Hellen to me.
Crucified with Augustine, Paul, and Nate
For just some pears we found drooping:
Over the gate.
The inferno ain't nothing I hate;
An angel to them but Francesca to me!

Hanging out underneath the marquis...
I'm three times cockier than you,
O set the stage voluntarily.
Bianca to you but Miranda for me.
Shot through the stars thinking I am
Doomed to miss.
Thought I'd burn up in the nebulaic mist.
Turns out the shot was worth the risk.
Etna Corina to you but Tarantula to me,
Supernova baby.

IV

One, two, one, two, three, four.

Now I'm just a punk and I don't know a thing about love but there's two kids I know and the word fits them like a glove and the there's a little cliché in the way they feel for each other but there's a little cliché in every time two people decide they love one another.

Joel and Shelby, Shelby and Joel, where'd you get the idea love is something you can control?

Shelby is eighteen and she's about to give birth to twins. And her boyfriend's named Joel and he doesn't judge her for it. He's just twenty-one and who is he to know what she's going in it for? Shelby tells Joel she's in love now, and she wasn't before.

Joel and Shelby, Shelby and Joel, where'd you get the idea love is something you can control?

Shelby's still in high school and Joel's mom was teaching her art. Joel lives down the street and that's as good a place as any to start. Joel started babysitting Shelby's kids while she went to school and Shelby noticed that when Joel was around she couldn't keep her cool.

Joel and Shelby, Shelby and Joel, where'd you get the idea love is something you can control?

Shelby said "Joel, baby I thought I was learning about love, but two kids later I don't know just what I was thinking of?"
Joel said "Shelby I think your body is magic! I'll be the father it don't have to be one bit tragic."

Joel and Shelby, Shelby and Joel, why do you think you're in love: it's out of your control.

And Shelby said: "I won't tell my mom about you if you don't tell your dad about me."

Now I've never been in love but there was Shelby asking up why she thought that if her and Joel weren't in love she'd just die? I said "Shelby you ain't got to worry about a thing. If you've come this far and you still want to be in love that's everything."

Joel and Shelby, Shelby and Joel, won't you show me love is something I can control? Something I can control.

Shelby! You're young enough to take my advice if you've got a chance at love then there's no time left to think twice. Your kids are like a boulder and you're graduating from school and if Joel is the one than I don't want you to act the fool.

So, take him to church, take him to bed, ask him about what his mom said, about all the paint you spilled in school and please Shelby don't lose your cool.

V

Lost report cards and lost islands
Stretched out fingers open eyelids
Baby boys, baby boys.
South sea playdates, silly playmates
Empty bottles, baby bibs
Baby boys, baby boys.

Telephone, hypomania, over stimulation:
Alright, alright. A bar fight you won.
Overthink, double thought, punk imagination:
You might, you might, pay for your fun.
Wooden dolls, plastic guns, water balloons if they ask me what I miss: it's you.

The Hamlet Express to Hamilton Ontario

Dear gentle reader,

My nickname is Young Bluebeard. Oh on my Canadian passport the name reads Hector Campbell. I'd bravely dealt with a nickname before and now I feel entitled to a new one so I've cajoled and insisted it's Young Bluebeard. Now that I'm out on my ass from college it's easy to get the guys to say what I want about me.

Right now it's Friday the twenty-first of December Twenty-Eighteen. I'm depleted of cigarettes and also my friend Gates will be along shortly to exchange one cut for another as is our custom. We're sorely addicted to Nicotiana Tobacco.

Exterior and Daytime, two past twelve in the Hamlet of Hamlet in the City of Hamlet. The last fall leaves are a mess on the ground.

Gates

I'm awake now but it's indeterminate. I sleep I wake and for who knows how long at a time. Don't pay attention anymore the computers are registering this and that these days. Nothing keeps me in bed like craving a cigarette and nothing gets me out of bed like craving a cigarette. I can always double down on Bluebeard cause if he hasn't got any to trade sure thing his father will have. What's more is that Bluebeard is a true friend and I'll insist his company at the movies tonight, this time I'll convince him.

In the residential boulevards of the Hamlet of Hamlet in Ontario the roads are lined with concrete sidewalks and broad lawns with trees overhanging as if the branches were leafy arcades. This year the chill of December is not sever. Gates has a majestic wide gait, strides across the dale and nimble, pricks into his phone even though he can already see his neighbor's garage where Bluebeard's father is standing.

Bluebeard (out of the telephone)
Gates friend, so glad to hear your ring-a-bell eager to meet my ear three sleeps before Christmas. I am pucker plain spent of cigarettes, eh?

Gates (to Bluebeard's father)
So, he's plain out of smokes again?

Bluebeard's Father
Guess so.

Bluebeard enters onto the scene of the wide and neighborly garage his father is tidying to meet Gates.

Bluebeard
Dad might I have a cig?

Bluebeard's Father
Not a chance go get your own.

Gates
That solves it you'll have to purchase.

Bluebeard
No error dad.

Bluebeard's Father
I never err son.

And Bluebeard and Gates are off striding into the lottery shop where Bluebeard posts an invoice printed off home-office software on the desk.

Bluebeard
How long have you slept Gates?

Gates
Long time, couldn't apply myself to any specific calculation but as long as landscaper's trade work is at a lull in the wintertime.

Bluebeard (with a rat-a-tat-tat shushes Gates)
A tat tat tat and do you think you sleep often and long in a deranged attempt to conserve on smoke?

Gates
Yeah, that's true.


Bluebeard

I've noticed the same in me, I'm languid and slopy and it's all this fool habit's fault but golly the smoke makes playing Crosswords more interesting.

Gates
Crosswords and Cutthroat, we played boardgames Wednesday with vivacity no civility in our vocabulary shoving the letters onto the board in every confirmation of a base and apish spirit in our brains.

Bluebeard
I took a picture of the results, we can laugh at the play for years to come.

Gates leans into the phone and sees Bluebeard's snapshot of the Crosswords board.

Gates
Nice. It's three sleeps before Christmas whatever they're getting you they should hurry I'd like to buy enough packs to last me until next Thursday now that you mention the lethargy.

Bluebeard
I want to quit.

The store attendant checks Bluebeard's chit and posts a case of twenty packs of five cigars a pack on the countertop for Bluebeard to take possession of.

Gates

Wow silly, you say you want to quit and yet, you've got your arms full of cigars. Merry Christmas!

Bluebeard
I hate and hate to smoke believe me it ails me. Dad smokes, uncles smoke, and everyone's got a marijuana habit I think. I'll get clean one day soon but well, I'd better had just learned medicine and manners by the time I was aged Twenty-One and caught myself before this abysmal addiction had gripped me. That's been nine years ago I am thirty now! I hated being twenty-one what a gutter year. If I go to the casino and someone tries to get my goat: hands me a pack of smoke, the slut walks over on my left and I'm gin-drunk that's when I'll know I have a winning hand.

Gates
Dang, and if all that comes true Scorch will amble up and say:

"Look guys, I'm all the way up max betting on the machines, guys I won money!"

Fork one of those tetra packs my way Bluebeard.

Bluebeard
No doubt the owing balance is in your favor, mind you I'm half in on this case with Scorch. This pack will have to come from my half.

Bluebeard forks over the smoke. Gates handles some change over to the clerk and they both emerge into the first day of winter with toasty smokes. They breath it in.

Gates
Do you think God exists?

Bluebeard
Yeah. Broccoli and the great jungle flowers from which our flowers are pale clippings, and the way of all things has a stem and a root. Cleave to it and on that highway of thought and deed there is lesser and greater. And of the greater and in deference to the lesser there is the greatest thing that can take root in practice. Maybe you think that's crazy and listen if I'm telling the truth that makes the two of us sort lousy.

Gates
Are we the demons? I think there is a heaven and a hell and we're the demons and what's worse is the devil is in the world.

Bluebeard
No. We're flowering buds, not counting for much but pollen, this smoke here is our blooming color. Gates I'm going home to giftwrap all these five-piece tetra packs of cigar.

Gates
These are some kind of Christmas present.

Bluebeard
They'll serve me dandy as a Christmas gift with my father's father's sons.

Gates
Thanks then. I've mulled over the picture of your face Bluebeard as if it was composed of ten thousand pixel pigments. You bere a lot of concern about your friends and family, I guess you really do believe in God.

Bluebeard
Well let's up the ante than! I'll let you know what I think of you two which is you're a majestic sort of strider but you need to acquire a sense of occasion Gates. Meet me at church on Christmas morning?

Gates
Sure I'll attempt it but no promises.

Bluebeard
Baptism! Holy Baptism Gates. See you there.

Gates
Hey do you ever think about what it would be like if we were truly brothers?

Bluebeard

Huh? You ever think of what it would be like to be in contest with my brother Achilles?

Gates
Point taken. Well fine then, I'll see you in church on Christmas day if only to bring some polish to your borrowed moto in my mind:

"Keep your arms and legs in the vehicle...

Bluebeard joins in.

"And all restraints fastened at all times during the ride." And you know why I borrowed that moto Gates?

Gate
Why?

Bluebeard
I like roller-coaters.

Gates
Oh that does it. Let's go to the movies. It's Friday first day of winter and there's blockbusters at the cinema!

Bluebeard
Movies try my patience and you try my patience at the movies the way you can't go through one without exiting the showroom for a cigarette.

Gates takes offence and before Bluebeard can deliver that last rebuke he's off into the dale speedy and as majestic as he appeared when he walked onto the premises which is Bluebeard's father's house.

Three sleeps later, Monday, Christmas Eve exterior on the boulevards outside Hamlet civic art gallery, the Hamlet of Hamlet.

An exhibition banner announces: A & A Elfsen, Impressionist Masters Opens January Twenty-Nineteen.

In the front of a medium-capacity transport truck Bluebeard's father parks the vehicle. The painters Adam Elfsen and Andrew Elfsen drive up the rear in a sedan with Bluebeard riding backseat. The truck door springs open and Bluebeard and father hoist one after another masterpiece painting out of the chassis and into the gallery for display.

Bluebeard
Uh, listen wait up before we're done here, I need to do a tad of banking up the street.

Bluebeard shuffles out of sight and glares at his accounts in aside. Two days prior his purchase of cigars had cost him two hundred and fifty dollars Canadian. Now, with trepidation he withdraws another three hundred dollars.

Bluebeard's Father

How much money did you fetch in total?

Bluebeard
Three hundred dollars.

Bluebeard's Father
Including Friday's purchase of cigars?

Bluebeard
Including that it would be more sort of like five hundred and fifty.

Bluebeard's Father
That's quite a lot!

Andrew Elfsen
What's all that money for?

Bluebeard
Some of it's for more gifts. I cannot tender my sisters cigars to smoke for Christmas. I'll need to spend a little and I should give to charity at mass.

Bluebeard's Father
What charity have you picked out?
Bluebeard
No research, I'll just do it through the church.

Adam Elfsen
Funny thing, Hector is always in church Mister Campbell but you are not.

Bluebeard's Father
I encouraged it when the boys were children now it's up to them. You understand Hecctor your brother Achilles is hosting the festivities in Hamilton this year and there is no time for church away from home.

Bluebeard
I didn't know, it didn't cross my mind. Things are fast-paced and thrilling this year.

Adam Elfsen
You two look dashing, really outstanding. I know you have a habit of doing Christmas shopping on Christmas Eve.

Bluebeard's Father
That's true. There's no way you want to get caught up at the telephone company on Christmas Eve or Christmas Day so I've booked it as a holiday ever since I had the quorum seniority I need to get it.

Bluebeard
Is it necessary to do the shopping in the nick of time each year dad?
Bluebeard's Father
What now? You might have shopped sooner, and you have. It's not as if you've been prescient with the chores your mom assigns either. I could leave you out. Furthermore, you've already wrapped the case of cigars and already you're itching to shop more. That's impulsive.

Bluebeard
You're right dad. Please don't dress me down in front of the brothers with this alacrity, I'm ashamed.

Bluebeard's Father
Well met, let's go. Say goodbye to the Elfsen's we'll park this truck and then scoot down to the Downtown Shopping Center in the car you and I.

No long later Bluebeard and Bluebeard's father are cruising towards Toronto Ontario on the Don Valley Parkway.

Bluebeard
I'll need a portion of this cash for the celebrations at the luchador match you assured me we'll see tonight, Christmas Eve.

Bluebeard's Father
Yes, yes we're going to see the luchadores and it's good you know I'd rather you tab your own bar bill. Don't even think about taking a solitary smoke from me. Not after you purchased a case of cigars.

Bluebear waves the tetra-pack of smoke.

Bluebeard
Right here and I'll pay for the beers I'd like.

Bluebeard's Father
Correct, and wise because I'm certain to slowly drink a pint after all the shopping's made me dizzy.

It rains and pours a heavy snow above Downtown Toronto. Bluebeard eats a sausage cart meal at city hall hop skipping east to the shopping center he whistles, earnestly he whistles, in melodic match to the shopping center PA Christmas tunes. Bluebeard's father crushes a cigarette and they both duck into the mall swallowed up into the sea of eager shoppers.

Day turns into evening as the two men purchase. Bluebeard stands at an engraver politely waiting on two pens he's bought: one with an angel, one with a heart for his sisters.

Bluebeard
Perfect, great. (He thanks the engraver.)

Bluebeard's Father
That's really top notch, engraved pens. I'm always impressed with the way you pick'em son. You manage to chose a top-flight item that makes me seem sort of shabby.

Bluebeard
If you mean to say I make you seem a poorer in refinement than I am, sure my spectacular eye for gifts makes you look second rate.

Bluebeard's Father

Son, I give you life, room, and board. Call me second rate a second time and I'll make things a bit miserable for you.

Bluebeard
Don't let me forget it dad. Now let's pack our things away and head towards a tavern.

Bluebeard's Father
The Duke's own pub is the type of restaurant that suits me best. Let's get the merchandise into the car.

In the upper level of the parking garage Bluebeard fumbles with a satchel that's waiting in the passenger's seat. It's brimming with gift wrapped cigars.

Bluebeard's Father
Put those down.

Bluebeard
Ah see, I've got to carry the half of them and I'll tell you why. Half these cigars are due to Scorch and I want Scorch to meet me at the luchador show. That being that I've got his cigars hostage.

Bluebeard's Father
If I hadn't seen he's a bright boy and strong I'd stop you but I like Scorch so you'll get away with this foolishness Hector.

Bluebeard and his father arrive at the Duke's pub. Bluebeard's father enters right away to make his order but Bluebeard sparks a cigar and stands out in the snow. He huffs and puffs the December sun sinks into night. "Scorch" Bluebeard pecks into his cell phone "You've promised to arrive here and the luchadores begin at eight-thirty. I hope you arrive on time."

Bluebeard enters the pub. When he walks out again it is after no less than two pints of beer drunk.

Bluebeard
We should take the streetcar.

Bluebeard's Father
You're drunk but I sip slowly and always mind my water intake. Line or traffic there's no avoiding a big crowd during the holiday. Good thing we're not shy and I'm a great driver.
In the Car again Bluebeard's Father scopes and strategizes how to park at the Great Hall where the line for the luchador match is spilling onto the sidewalk.

Bluebeard's Father
Now, don't you go bumming cigarettes off total strangers at the event.

Bluebeard
My pack is right here, but, if I so chose to trade a stranger his cigarette for my cigar that's not a bad

trade. Otherwise they wont be strangers because of course they'll be ticket holders to the great luchador match.

Bluebeard steps into the staircase of the Great Hall which is crowded with people. To the nearest gentlemen on the staircase Bluebeard nods and injures:

Bluebeard
Is this the ticket holder's line?

Ticket Holder
Yup, this is the line.

Bluebeard
I see you're smoking. Merry Christmas have a cigar.

Bluebeard's father is out of site the snow drifts heavy and white everywhere into slushpuddles and snowbanks and the sidewalk is busy with festival.

Bluebeard
Hector don't miss an instant of this day.

As Bluebeard's Father checks through the box office gate and rounds onto the staircase disorderly and slow as it is Bluebeard is almost going to follow when over his shoulder he sees a sight. Jamaica Dennett is at the top of the staircase.

Bluebeard

Dennett! Merry Christmas Jamaica!

Jamaica
Oh man, it said you would be here and you're here, the internet is so cool.

Bluebeard
I know the internet said you would be here and here you are. It's so nice when old friends see one another.

Jamaica
You've stayed in touch with city slicker.

Bluebeard
You would know. I have and I act like I have.

Jamaica
I always hope to see someone else here at his shows.

Bluebeard
They don't know, they don't know. It's not important, I come to see him so do you, it's not like absentees are going to break his heart. I mean think of the cardio he does. Hey, remember he always used to call me by that nickname? My friends gave me a new nickname.

Jamaica
You have a new nickname. I'm impressed S-------

Bluebeard whinnies with disapproval a guffaw and a finger to his lips.

Bluebeard
I don't like it, it's embarrassing, and all those years City Slicker still finds it a joy.

Jamaica
You could always stop coming to his shows.

Bluebeard
It's not like that's going to break his heart.

Jamaica
Well the new nickname, what is it?

Bluebeard
Young Bluebeard.

Jamaica
That's not a rap name is it?

Bluebeard
It can be:

I'm powerful/power this/weed wacker in a power grip/ axes on my back and in my taxes/ I back shit/ come at me with wack shit/ attack this? / facts is your batshit.

Bluebeard pauses and frowns at his own fumbling with the rap manner.

Bluebeard
It's not a rap name, it's just, you know a nick name.

Jamaica
Hmph. Was Bluebeard the one who was locked in the closet?

Bluebeard
Bluebeard was the one who kept his closet locked.

The luchador match begins. The rounds go by. Finally Scorch dials Bluebeard on his cell phone.


Scorch (Out of the cell phone microphone)
Oh my God. Oh my God. Hey, hey bro. Sorry I'm so late getting here downtown, but you know I got the herb, the cigars and I'm here with my boo.

Bluebeard
You brough Little Starlight! Perfect. I'm telling you though, you need to be here for this match between the two top fighters. City Slicker and King Lu, King of Kung Foo.

Scorch
I'm going to bet on King Lu, King of Kung Foo.

Bluebeard

You know, most people don't bet on fixed wrestling matches.

Scorch
Sure, but do you know the outcome?

Bluebeard
No.

Scorch
So bet me a lottery ticket the Kung-Foo guy won't win. I'll be here soon, wait, wait for me.

Bluebeard
I'm already here dude. It's just up to you if you're going to show up or not.

Scorch
I'm coming. What do you say? One lottery ticket. We can play it in the shop together a few days from now.

Bluebeard
I don't know Scorch people might think we're crazy for betting on fixed matches. But, you know what, yes. I only need to buy a lottery ticket.

Jamaica trails Bluebeard out of the hall onto the block.

Jamaica
We've got company.

Bluebeard
True that.

Diamond and Tall Ginger Simon get out of a streetcar, gliding over the snow and onto the street in front of The Great Hall and out of the rear car of the same vehicle come tumbling Scorch and Little Starlight!

Bluebeard
This is astonishing. Have any of you seen City Slicker wrestle prior to now?

Simon
I haven't

Scorch
Way no way!

Diamond
Nope.

Little Starlight
Let's get inside.

Bluebeard
He's quite acrobatic.

Jamaica
Very acrobatic.

Bluebeard

The show has begun so he won't come out of the dressing rooms until his entrance for sure now. But wait, Jamaica, what draws these guys here? I've got a satchel of cigars I've used to bribe my friends.

Bluebeard begins forking half the satchel of tetrapacks of smoke over to Scorch.

Jamaica
We're attending Graduate School together, Simon, Diamond, City Slicker and I all applied for Graduate School in Film and Television. We've been accepted to the upcoming class. It's not something we planned out. We have been working at different schools but as things turned out what we wanted to do was- S-

Bluebeard
Whoa whoa please don't call me that.

A tear rolls down Bluebeard's face.

Bluebeard
I understand I'll get it together one day to. Sorry, ah, sorry guys.

Scorch
Bluebeard where's your dad?

Little Starlight
We should go stand with your dad.

Bluebeard
Of course, he's on the ground level. We'll pick this up after the match. Please.

Simon
Of course we will. You can bribe us with cigars.

Scorch
Bet.

City Slicker makes his wrestling entrance and plays the heel to the crowd. He sings a Christmas song from the public register and berates his opponent Kung Foo King Lu as being a Scrooge. King Lu takes genuine offence, and the match begins.
Slam after slam the roar of the crowd is all behind City Slicker the hometown Adonis. Scorch and Little Starlight eye it all with giddy thrill they paste their surprise to their faces. Bluebeard watches with an eye of concern whenever his friend takes gets chopped thrown clotheslined or slammed.

Outdoors after 'City Slicker' stands in the parking lot with Simon, Diamond, Scorch, Little Starlight, Jamaica, Bluebeard and Bluebeard's father.

Bluebeard
City Slicker, meet Scorch and this is Little Starlight. Scorch, City Slicker.

Scorch

Pleased to meet you. All of you, so nice to meet you. Say, what do you think we make tonight a Santa Clause Parade.

City Slicker
I'm wiped, tired, busted and beat I tell you. So. I do have to say no to the smoke. It's a delight to see you all, a very delight. I feel like a genuine Kris Kringle. Diamond! Simon! And Little Starlight?

Little Starlight
That's me. At first we didn't bet on you.


City Slicker
You know these matches are fixed?

Scorch
Did Bluebeard know that? See I was just making a bet and then I walked in and you wrestled so intensely, pow-pow, because I thought that the Kung Foo guy would win, naturally.

City Slicker
Naturally, but tonight was my night to win.

Bluebeard
All a part of the meta narrative of the sport of luchadores?

City Slicker
Coin toss.

As City Slicker who has taken the thrashing of all time from his opponent King Lu, leaves the event whose attendance he's gathered he gives hearty hugs to Jamaica and Bluebeard and handshakes to everyone else.

City Slicker
God Bless.

Bluebeard's Father
I am to understand Scorch and Little Starlight are both coming to Hamilton with us tonight?

Little Starlight
Not me, I have to be back in Hamlet to manage the café. It will be open Christmas day.

Bluebeard
And father, Scorch and I are actually not coming to Hamilton Ontario just this instant.

Bluebeard's Father
What was that I heard about making tonight a Santa Clause Parade?

Jamaica
That's true. Merry Christmas. We're partying, see, Simon, Diamond and I have made a pact to go on to graduate school and it's time for the pub crawl.

Bluebeard is surprised. The promises have weighed in and deranged his mind by now. How can he have a Santa Clause Parade with Scorch and be at Church with Gates, and make it to dinner in Hamilton?

Bluebeard's Father
Don't be late to Christmas you hear?

Bluebeard
Goodbye dad. Go to Hamilton. I'll be at my brother's house for Christmas.

Bluebeard's Father drives off and away into the snow. Scorch enters the nearby lottery shop and fetches the lottery ticket he owes Bluebeard.

Diamond
Are you all ready to tramp it through the snow?

Simon
With this much smoke we can stay toasty.

Little Starlight
But what's our destination?

Diamond
There's many sights and sound between here and Museum Subway Station which, by the way, has sarcophagus in the train bay.

Little Starlight
Tremendous.

Scorch
Funny thing, I celebrate Christmas but I'm a Hindu. I don't know much about it, just, it's a great party.

Diamond
Let me tell you something about Christmas: Jesus Christ changed the world.

Simon
Some would say not for the better.
Diamond
Well enough for the stoic to say.

Scorch
What? You don't like Christmas? I don't know but to inference from the festivities I'm pretty sure Jesus wasn't a bad guy.

Simon
Oh no it's nothing personal, it's only, with his perfectionism he tore apart the stoic ideal.

Scorch
Stoicism, Bluebeard, you know about that.

Bluebeard
That's right, stoicism was the dominant philosophical school during the period the Roman Empire ruled the world.

Diamond

For the better.

Simon
So says a thrashed eudaemonist?

Scorch
Eudaimonism, that's someone who just wants to be happy right?

Diamond
Simply put, yes.
Simon
We all just want to be happy.

Diamond
But we go about it in different ways. I'm surprised you're following so well Scorch.

Simon
Everyone this time of year talks about Christmas, Jesus Christ! But what they should really focus on is another man, Julius Caesar.

Scorch
Who's that like Santa Clause?

Diamond
I see we lost you.

Scorch
Just kidding I know Julius Caesar to, there's a stage play named after him.

Simon
Julius Caesar was a Roman general and then, the Emperor of Rome and a stoic. What he thought was that happiness is about security, that if you could build the walls and defend the city then everyone would have enough peace to make their happiness come true.

Diamond
But then this Messiah came along not sixty years after Old Man Caesar had proved his point by becoming ruler of the Roman Empire.

Simon
Oh give it a rest or I'll rip your kid gloves right off Diamond.

Scorch
Whoa. Caesar sounds like he was a happy guy until Jesus came along.

Diamond considers Simon's threat in jest and sucks his teeth but then continues for the benefit of all and Scorch.

Diamond
Not exactly, he was assassinated by being stabbed thirty-three times by members of the Roman Senate. But that's not what's a stake. The issue is, if Jesus hadn't come along I think the point would have been

met. Become king, rule strongly, make peace, bring security, and everyone lives better.

Simon
And sure, that sounds alright. But funny thing is people don't become happy in little pieces. The eudaemonist said, believes, that happiness is like a puzzle that you need to get all the pieces right to.

Diamond
Hoh, describe it that way and I don't see why you have trouble with Jesus who just painted a picture for the puzzle everyone was trying to put together.

Simon
And the crucifixion among other notable notes?

Scorch
Okay what you're saying is that people must have agreed on how to be happy once Julius Caesar was Emperor but then Jesus did things differently. What was so different about Jesus.

Diamond
Lots. Jesus wanted everyone to be perfect.

Scorch
I don't know about being perfect I just want to be good.

Simon
Well if you want to be good then you'll have no problem being perfect because Jesus said they're the same thing.

Scorch
At first Julius Caesar sounded boss but you know what, I imagine I like Jesus better now. It's a Christmas miracle.


Bluebeard
You see Robarts library over that way?

Jamaica
A brutal place, in there I can get just trampled by everything I know I don't know just have to browse the stacks.

Bluebeard
Yea, but you've got to go I to see what it's got I recommend it. Let me tell you a story about Robarts library. Once upon a time I was in the foyer there on the second floor and some poor sparrow had flown into the space and was trapped inside. I was a sweat from my commute, and I felt I knew the bird so I watch it flutter up high, swoop down low and peck about on the ground until eventually I caught it in between my palms. That was the moment I realized it's the dead of winter. As I let it outside, I could feel it's heartbeat race, I knew it had a frequency and I understood just how bittersweet civilization really is.

Jamaica comes close to Bluebeard as they walk.

Jamaica
You aren't walking with little starlight.

Bluebeard
She's Scorch's boo. How are things with City Slicker.

Jamaica
It's like in a computer simulation, the more he tries, the tougher the stakes.

Jamaica kisses Bluebeard on the cheek.

Bluebeard
Mmm, don't do that again.

The group arrives at Museum Station Subway

Bluebeard
Alright parade this is where we split into contingents?

Diamond and Simon, Scorch did not witness Jamaica kiss Bluebeard, but Little Starlight did.

Little Starlight
You've told me the station is worth touring and you must be right. There's glitz in the air all around this quarter where are we?

Diamond
Well Mademoiselle we're at the corner of University and Bloor, Yorkville is directly to the East.

Scorch
There's pot shops in Yorkville!

Bluebeard
You check your phone and see if there's anything near and the five of us will tour the sarcophagus in the train station.

Diamond, Simon, Jamaica and Young Bluebeard and Little Starlight head into the underground.

Little Starlight
This is quite as marvelous as the glitz above ground here.

Simon
Oh golly, the train arriving right on time.

Bluebeard
Oh gosh I think this must be the final time we all see each other.

Jamaica
Don't believe that it's not true.

The train hurtles into the station and in a wink the doors spring wide. In goes Simon, in goes Diamond, in goes Jamaica Dennett.

Jamaica
Au revoir.

Bluebeard
Au secour au revoir!

Simon
Au revoir

Diamond
Au revoir

Little Starlight
Bye.

The train whooshes away. The station is still and empty. Young Bluebeard looks at his shoes and then remembering Gates majestic gait he poses like a dancer and mimes a waltz. Grinning at Little Starlight he takes her in his arms and they waltz and they waltz and dizzy they crash into the sarcophagus pillars.

Little Starlight
She kissed you.

Bluebeard
Yea.

**Little Starlight**
I should kiss you.

**Bluebeard**
No you shouldn't.

**Little Starlight**
Too late.

**Bluebeard**
Let's go get Scorch we are going to take the very next southbound train to Union Station.

Bluebeard runs up the station steps.

**Bluebeard**
Come back outside Little Starlight we'll pay the fair again.

Outside the museum Station Scorch is smoking up, he's traded cigars for French fries out in the cold.

**Scorch**
I made a friend. Her name's Emma.

**Emma**
It was the gift wrap that caught my eye. I like a well wrapped Christmas gift.

The dashing Emma seems to have taken Scorch for quite a few tertrapacks of smoke.

Bluebeard
What brings you about here on Christmas eve.

Emma
I'm in Fashion at the Yorkville Shopping Center I'm just making my way back to my apartment.

Bluebeard
Bookstore?

Emma
The art shop.

Bluebeard
Splendid I'm working on my watercolors.

Scorch
Did you know Norm McDonald Published a book?

Emma
Are you related of something.

Scorch
He makes me laugh my ass off like an uncle.

Bluebeard
The three of us have got to get to Union Station again. This is a clear sign the shops are closed, there's no more use in our Santa Clause Parade.

Scorch

I could stay out all night.

Little Starlight
No you really can't.

Bluebeard
Let's go. Nice to meet you Emma, so long.
 Exterior at the Union Station Bus Terminal

Bluebeard
Oh gosh oh gosh. It's Gates on the phone.

Gates
Are we going to Church tomorrow dude?

Scorch
Haha, yeah you promised Gates you'd go to Church with him tomorrow. But you can't.

Bluebeard
Unless I can. I promised the three of those guys I'd be at church. Gates, Andrew and Adam. And I want to. My family doesn't actually realize that I'm deeply religious. I want to be in church tomorrow.

Little Starlight
Somebody has escort me home to the café right?

Scorch
Mademoiselle

Little Starlight

I mean Bluebeard should do it. And you Scorch go along to Christmas acting like a full decoy! You'll be able to get back to Hamilton in time Bluebeard you just need to take an Express bus middy.

Bluebeard
That wouldn't not work. Scorch can you decoy?

Scorch
No. I can't how can I face your brother Achilles?

Bluebeard
That's true. Well let me write a letter. That could solve it, you'd be my messenger, and no one shoots the messenger.

Scorch
Are you certain.

Little Starlight
If you don't go now you'll miss out on the Christmas Dinner because someone's got to escort me back to Hamlet.

Scorch
Right. So let me get it all worked out strait, what I'm hearing is if worst comes to worst your portion of the dinner is mind Bluebeard.

Bluebeard
If I don't make it, eat my food and you take back the lottery ticket.

Scorch
That makes sense and god oh man, here's the express bus to Hamilton.

Bluebeard
Get on the bus please.

Scorch
Alright. See you soon man, meet me in Hamilton tomorrow or your brother will crush my bones to make his cupcakes, lol.

The Express Bus to Hamilton pulls forwards and away.

Little Starlight
Can I have your cigar?

Bluebeard
No.

Little Starlight
You don't have anyone.

Bluebeard
Scorch has you Starlight. That's his hopes and dreams. We're going to Hamlet and you will not share my cigar and you will not kiss me again.

And in a whisper Little Starlight says: "Too late."

Exterior Daytime on Christmas Morning. The Hamlet of Hamlet, City of Hamlet, Ontario.

Gates
Merry Christmas Bra.
Bluebeard
Are you coming to church?

Gates
I don't suppose you'd let me score cigars any other way?

Bluebeard
You could buy your own.

Gates
I got packs I'll trade you.

The rapscallions enter the Church of Saint Anthony.

The reverend preaches on Christmas morning.

Gates and Bluebeard quietly scooch into a pew beside the senior Mr. Elfsen, but surprise he's alone in the pew.

Adam Elfsen
Hector, Reginald. Merry Christmas.

Bluebeard

What are you doing with that cell phone. I've never seen you use the telephone outside of the shop before.

Adam Elfsen
Well, my brother is supposed to be here, but I can't seem to find him after we were at the coffee house for breakfast.

Gates
Does he even have a phone to reach by?

Adam Elfsen
No. It's this Christmas crowd. We often make our way to church singly but the crowd is overwhelming on Christmas Day.

Gates
Don't worry Mr. Elfsen we'll scout this place in all quarters to find Andrew. You can simply pay attention to the mass.

Bluebeard
Where have you told your brother to meet you.

Adam Elfsen
At Saint Anthony's. Here.

Bluebeard
That's not so specific Adam, there are two Saint Anthony's Churches on this Main Street of the

Hamlet of Hamlet Ontario, not to mention Charity Anglican and Saint Brendan's Catholic.

Adam Elfsen
He might have got turned around that's true.
Gates and Bluebeard observe the heavy press of the crowd around them and grimace at the idea of picking out Andrew from the bustle.

They scooch out of the pew and search high and low, failing that Gates and Bluebeard depart the first Saint Anthony's and move to the second building of the same patronage up the street.

Gates spots Andrew Elfsen and he and Bluebeard scooch in next to him.

Gates
We've been looking for you brother. Your brother is at Saint Anthony's.

Andrew Elfsen
This is Saint Anthony's.

Bluebeard
The other Saint Anthony's.

Andrew Elfsen
I see that's embarrassing should be leave.

Bluebeard

I'm in no rush. In for a minute in for an hour with these sort of things and if we miss the other Saint Anthony's they're going to run the service again today as it's Christmas Day.


Gates
But it's my wish we make hast to the Catholic Church. They have the most beautiful church.

Andrew Elfsen
Because they have the most money.

Bluebeard
Who knows it might be vice versa.

The three rapscallions scooch out of the Saint Anthony's Church and get moving in the direction of Saint Anthony's Church, which are not the same church. They encounter Adam Elfsen.

Adam Elfsen
Of terrific, well we're heading to Charity Anglican.

Bluebeard
That's just the spot I wished to donate my tithe, but I haven't. Can't I put it in your hands Adam Elfsen?

Adam Elfsen
Well I suppose so.

Bluebeard forks over a portion of a hundred dollars for donation at Charity Anglican.

Gates
But why are we parting ways now?

Andrew Elfsen
It's alright for young whippersnappers like you fellas to get caught in the overwhelming crowds at Catholic Church on Christmas Morning, not for us thanks.

Bluebeard and Gates stride merrily down the block from Saint Anthony's and a short distance the walk down the highway to Saint Brendan's Catholic.

Bluebeard
Not a trace of a fib that's a crowd like you're likely to see at a baseball game in the lot of Saint Brendan's.

Gates
The papists who run the spectacle have their share of trouble today and on Easter it never fails.

Exterior in Hamilton, it's two past noon.
Achilles Campbell and his spouse Cleo stand on their apartment balcony scanning the streetscape for signs of guest.

Cleo
Do you think everyone will be late.

Achilles
I hadn't expected my father to be early, he's gone to buy the drinks but tell me Hector is due in an instant.
Cleo
Did you hear about the new nickname he's got his friends calling him. Bluebeard. I bet it's his rap name.

Achilles
I don't know.

Cleo
Oh wow, look at that guy with the cigar in his chompers. I think he's dancing. Yell out to him.

Achilles
I will. Yo! I heard the government is going to ban smoking!

Scorch
Yo! Achilles! I heard it's the other way around smoking is going to try and ban the government. I have a letter from your brother Bluebeard Achilles, a Christmas card.

Achilles
This cannot be ideal. How did it come to this a jolly man with a cigar brings bad news down my chimney on Christmas day?

Scorch enters the house and emerges on the balcony.

Achilles
The letter says and I read: Dear Achilles, I am going to church this morning. I am very sorry for the heartache my absence might have cause to effect. I just feel strongly about church, about my connections in Hamlet, I've been unwell lately as you know. I think that I will catch the Hamlet Express to Hamilton Ontario soon after you get this letter. Please take care of my friend Scorch.

Achilles
What a kick in the teeth I'm furious. And he sent you Scorch. What a jack ass I'm going to call him and tell him not to bother coming at all.

Scorch
Don't do that. He's exhausted we were out dancing all night.

Achilles
What do you mean you were out dancing all night?!

At that moment in a roar a hemi truck pulls onto the block and out steps Heracles Campbell who is a measure bigger than Achilles.

Heracles
Whoa you look pissed Achilles, chill. Have you been into the beers already?

Achilles

Not at all Hector is still three hours away from the party in Hamlet.

Heracles
There's nothing we can do about it and you seem to be making his guest a bit uncomfortable. Who are you Hector's boyfriend?

Scorch
I'm a friend who's a boy but no.

Cleo
Now you've made him uncomfortable. Would you like a cupcake Scorch?

Scorch
Would I ever!

Finally Bernice Campbell pulls up on her motorcycle.

Bernice
You two look bad and mad.

Achilles
Hector is in Hamlet right now and I'm calling him to tell him to stay there. He hasn't sent any word until this instant with his messenger Scorch that he will be late for Christmas.

Scorch
Calm down guys just have a cigar.

Bernice
You know Hector is rather reserved about the telephone, and now it's apparent he is chronically religious. Please whatever you do don't cut into him over the air waves, he'll be rattled and then he won't make it.

Heracles
But if you keep it cool and say, make Scorch his boyfriend do the talking, he'll be at the party by dinner time.

Achilles
I can tell you're right. Scorch make it to be sure Hector is on the next Hamlet Express to Hamilton Ontario.

Exterior Hamlet of Hamlet, Three in the Afternoon.

Bluebeard
I feel lousy, I feel like I gummed it all up.

Gates
You've been waving that scratch card around all morning do you know how to use it?

Bluebeard
Not a clue.
Gates
Let's go in the shop and play your scratch card it will calm your nerves.

Bluebeard
I only want to sleep not to take the Hamlet Express to Hamilton Ontario.

Gates
You can sleep on the bus.

Bluebeard
No way it's going to be a long uncomfortable ride.

Gates
That's true of course.

Bluebeard
It will be crowded, lurching, smelly and slow.

Gates
No error. No error. Wait a moment no error, look at this card Bluebeard you won, you won money.

Bluebeard
Enough to take a taxi to Hamilton.

Gates
It's a dues-ex-machina.

"Winner GANGNANT!" The prize machine salutes.
Bluebeard
Yeah a dues-ex-machina. And if I keep my hands and legs inside the vehicle and all restraints fastened at all times during this taxi ride I'll make Hamilton by Five in the afternoon.

Gates
Well we better keep all this church stuff up and the miracles will keep on rolling.

End

My Darling's voice is nothing like the spheres
Orbiting carelessly forever them.
Toy my whole mind with their whimsy them
Her voice careers against a thousand hems

And carries me to distant ways.
It peels and tokes and surprises to see any trace of
melody
Her eyes cratered like the moons face, bright
Her Jupiter regret, her Saturn a glory
Lights that you would like to win
Have nothing hot as her mercury.
To have one more season about her.
To have another blissful shot at us
When the rest glee to see her zigzag
I'll say to all of them "you paid her dust".

The thought of love is apt to wax and wane
As long as your love is just out of reach
I will stay wise, courageous, just and sane
And pretend there's no fifth element to teach
Perfidiously profess the stoic view
Happiness is just craft for the fashion
The world is one there's no such thing as two
Put love on the list of wretched passions.
Perhaps you would not need an explanation about
the gloss
Perhaps you've seen it proved in cases of terror
Class love as a sport of catch and toss
Hush their lips and validate the error
I'd teach philosophy but not its source
If your love passes by me in its course.

The human heart is not a toy or game
Though it can be boxed it has every means to be free
By fates too offer unshelved just the same
Then reshelved by some godly O-C-D
If, like cobblers, the surgeons knew better
How to sew the fabric of the pumps
Fates would bat them even more like balls of leather
And send them back to God as bloody stumps!
Sometimes by vicious conscience, sometimes grace
I whirl around to catch life's meaning say,
While fate pops off a bleeding heart to see the look on my face
I have strength to be played and say it's fine
Knowing your heart was once shelved next to mine.

When mind's alight with landscapes weird and strange
Believing what a sober thought would crush
Through wind, earth, fire, and water I may range
When you appear in dreams it is a rush!
The indoor spaces huge, outdoors enclosed
Take flight by sunbeam and ski roof to roof
Surging' fants'y to outpace Lethe's flows
In sleep, to dream, we bargain away the truth.
Inevitably remembering fails in dreams
Reverie plot chase and tryst always collapse.
What do these lawless phantom shades redeem
That I will oversleep to have them last?
Agency (!) left intact would make me sue:
When I kiss you in dreams you kiss me to.

If I'm in love it begs the question how?
With so much reproof in my history
Solitude is familiar to me now
What insight could resolve the misery
Of shadows in church and confused parents at
home?
Villains to tenderness and cheer
My eyes color washing to monochrome
And loneliness becoming my great fear.
Only to be met with love in a maze
A gauntlet of hurdles, a bonafides test
But when I recall the slant of your gaze
I imagine your heart has not suffered less.
I'll spare you the drama and provide you the clue:
If I'm in love it's because I love you.


I'm sipping rye in little splashes
The way I've learned to drink church wine
My heart beats poetic dots and dashes
My spirit ascends the treacherous incline
Your context all rapid transition
And mine just antique violence
In absurd travail I'll change positions
To discover love where doubts are silenced.
From my doggy dale to your high peak
No territory daunts my ardent quest
Fame, limelight, and foregoing life that's meek
What seemed like sins, now altitudes to test.
Please excuse these small cold sips of liquor.
I just got drunk to make the journey quicker.

Where buildings' shadows cool my walking frame
I speed my gait to step where sunlight thrusts
From cool to warm then on through cool again
In fall when longer nights beguile my lusts.
Why won't the earth stand plumb strait as a spruce
Whose brawny center never changed direction
Can God do nothing for a cricket spoke
About the pinnacle of her invention?
That all is just but just the best is fair
(The ethicists' most outrageous conceit)
For sun and starlight raze the city bare
And say it wasn't best being incomplete.
By winter what could stills and fears
Except to say your name and see you here?

The game of words, so much a dungeon now
Was one a palace, gallery, and woods
The charmed cant of tales handed down
Now carved in stone verse and understood
As property not to be plagiarized
Originality, once loyal mount
Now a chimera monstrous and wise.
These labyrinth walls my love's talent surmounts.
Belatedly she'll rein as queen of song
Winning herself the ancient crown of lyric
In conquest her movements are never wrong
So I'll play mage and conjure sonnets' spirit
And capture words I write to win her favor
That her words touch my soul: the prize I savor.

Twelve hundred years into the kingdoms growth
Two haughty sprites were promoted to gods
When to Athena was Plutos betrothed
Daughter Folly adopted against the odds.
Unending wedding chime of bank desk bells
Made Athena feel a bride made richer
And in a vault of double entry cells
Daughter Folly hidden from the picture.
Eight centuries: the union might dissolve
Justice jilted by Wealth's unwise gambles.
Folly avariciously heir to all
Made golden hearts capacities scramble.
The era's bleak but by the love you render
Your heart outshines the ancient gods of tender.

That liberty is battle and the prize
Notwithstanding innocence in youth
Nothing less is worthy of your thighs
How well you have exegeted the truth.
Do not let them say children have it best
Or how they hid from war to protect them
All lovers pull ahead from all the rest
And naiveite in love you show defective.
A much as babes are wrapped against the noise
Like time capsules to a future strange and hot
I know you'd rather freedom then some boy
Let's hear your songs and believe you're not caught.
Of all the destinies you've run aground
Find in me scoundrel solace and a clown.

Where rats and kittens somehow doubt to play
On the heel of my pinky finger
There's no pet to command to sit or stay
No exotic serpent come to linger.
Eight eyed spider did not adapt to me
I've never owned a pup to train and test
No bottled flies or incubated bees
Insects often accused in girlish jests
The bugs die chasing each other in the window
wells
And I supposed my nervous wrist's relieved
That it's not clawed by feathered ne'er do wells.
As quiet as a pet I'll be believed...
My hearts' menagerie is indexed better
Not missing touch of fur or feather.

Don't I make it seem like luck's been played
A masterwork and fashioned so unfair
But other poets must not be dismayed
Here's some advice to get you halfway there:
Thorny opinion or the prose you bare
Cut each thing in two and what's left in two
Of a thing of maps from there to here
To get a quarter isometric view
Of arrogance and faithlessness
With all the gems of your memory spent
Don't swerve from your regrets and tastelessness
Then examine the marrow and repent.
Bleed from your pen the things you maybe said
Overcome the fear you might just bleed red.

Don't entertain doubts on my strength of nerve
Or put me down as novice to limelight
My poise on the slope of a learning curve
Is trained, on stage, and ready for a fight.
Notoriety leads only to abusing
(And here's the crux of why you need me dear)
I don't find the tabloids are amusing
I'd like to reduce each page to a torn smear.
With a smirk and a wink I'd fit into your set
Grinning, count myself worth a thousand words
Whether to drink or to casino, bet
I can't make your adventures seem absurd.
What seems absurd is every time I plea:
"Leave your boyfriend, spend some time with me."

Shake this picture and it will expose
The instance will be printed crisp and clear
A searching eye that happens on even my prose
Will not mistake the truth of friendship here.
The odd development of my intention
As if in thirteen frames of storyboard
Just to strange to strike home as invention
A scene to leave the tritest viewer floored.
All that's left's to label at the bottom
Eleven letters spelling out your name
Bragging to Twain authors that you've caught them
Pauper or princess you've been loved the same.
Show this heart I think they'll fear you toyed
Is just as dear to you as Polaroid.

I would wail and shout if long deprived
Of wheat of devils shit, yes nicotine
I smoke, am sick, then past sickness I writhe
I smoke, so sure to die, I'll die obscene.
Fired by the roll or firmed by my stress
Firm cigarette sticks or soft cigar
It's the worst so, purchased, begged the best.
Yet, more addicted to you then the tar.
If I was writhing you would hold me still
Willing and shouting curses, devils stuff
Past sickness, shinning, alight: needing thrills
If you were here to thrill me I'd not puff.
How awfully I feel I'm deceived of hope
I quench my spiritual fire with corporeal smoke.


That words will change and twist your mind no
doubt
That shouts square with echoes makes you dread
Culture reads and reading comes to shouts
Much more at risk to deafening: those who've read.
With the world seeming speaking to boast
On too novel English, too little loved
For syntax who committed to farther coasts?
From this high bank who parses depth from ford?
Used applied and researched, found quite young
Healthful as high hard breasts, as matrix womb
No credit goes to my English tongue
Listen it's not popular cause English booms!
So much for the cosmopolitan myth
Saying much about these words but not in pith.

Sunshine! Without you I wouldn't rise to see
Views of the star pouring it's warmth on dew
Last birdsong of twilight, new buzzing bees
Each morning that I have I have from you.
In starlight strolls I often roam the night
Alone among some inconsistent friends
Who I would treat much better if they might
Help pass the boredom your nightie absence sends.
Envious of me and my lovers' joys
Cough intelligence and my strength repellant
Those who treat their friendships as just toys
Awake maybe, but nightie seems a hell.
Never sorted in with fickle friends
I'm happy for each dawn sunshine portends.


If I tried sorting affirmations received
Into two groups: affirming and inferring
And logically draw out what I believe
Just the consideration sets me purring.
The outer rite a loan debt and a sorrow
Though I like it more than what's the news
Sane, I won't conflate now with tomorrow
Crazy, I price the ride and shoot for you.
I see conditioning in loyalty
I see a game of merit and of worth
Take all the time that this is going to take
A tragic roll for you, me foil (mirth).
I set my arm against the jests you turn
To achieve the wheels rebel love might earn.

Pleasures pleasuring simply cause they sell
To buy what pleases and to work to buy
Splendors, luxuries, sights sounds and smells
My palate for these things is just parched dry.
Trafficked grunts and gossips greedy talk
Good humoredly I tend to each as such
I might rally companions for a walk
But these are foolish guys that don't count much.
Of all the vapid unambitious miles
I like to think myself above the shame
They aren't pleased with spectacles or dope
I'm not pleased with things I know are drains
All these hedonist things I've turned away
So much more cynical should be our play.

I rush to the side of honest belief
Wherever skeptics tear at virtues' myths
Progress the fants'y graded or steep
I'll take virtue clothes and facts dealt with remiss.
I come with bookshop credits for criticism
Returned and repossessed for such fractional price
I am well experienced with mysticism
And I would gladly take Chinese advice:
Shining with daring, passionate and free
Do away with wooden social framework
Of the graded chairs of ancient philosophy
The structure of the words is surely good.
Pursuing what pursued is weirdly close
I'll close with words the issue that I boast.

Love isn't something you can control
It's a daring exchange of duties
It's assistance abreast a patrol
Maybe a phantom philological sum
And non-instrumentally posed
It follows its own course and judgment process.
Uphold the marriage codes like the plumbing faucet:
Crazy, cruel, metallic, money blue
I fear it more than I suppose it's nice
If it were not I am in love with you
I will take love as a subject on to think twice.
To love may seem a cure to distant ills
But romance today has demolishing thrills.

My breath is tight, my ears are pricked
Politely I asked, you pinched out the flame
Your denials: trite, your name's a trick
This conversation is driving me insane.
You dodge the point, I steal past your defense
You plunge towards love in extreme
Happily I follow though the subject's dense
Happily I say this nightmare is a dream.
The strain of a heavy hearted love
Stress my body and pulls my mind taught
If you thought I'd not been tempered enough
The steel of my intentions has you caught.
Though the force of what you wish is like a ton
I promise my heart will not be undone.

To this man what's abundantly clear
Is that man is damn out of place
When man isn't using his mirror
To look his desires in the face.
What's this thing I'm calling a mirror
This conceit, this poem, this device
Is it medicine, ethics and math
(Some subject that makes me think twice?)
The mirror is something called love
When I look in the glass I see you
Whether mirror of word, nerve, or chrome
When I approached the image grew.
There's nothing I couldn't be
If you looked in the mirror and saw me.

The life of a mirror is unnerving
Brittle: breaking one signals bad luck
But to pretend, paint face, or drive swerving
A mirror halves the risk, is worth the fuss.
Sometimes a glass smooth round perfected
But not necessarily a Chrome's backed glaze
Sometimes what's a mirror (on reflection)
Is the lattice nerve work of a face.
Your beauty is shinning, ornamental
Heel, clavicle, brow, you beguile
Your smile that was once temperamental
Is now etched straight and proud by trial.
When that face of yours smiling bends
The life of my broken nerves mends.

Really sort of thrifty for a rich boy
With words sort of common for his touch
In a city that is more like a father than a toy
A twinkle in his eyes and the stars as such.
This poem might relay what you need to hear
About the star girl that has thieved my heart
But about the boy that she has by the ear
I don't know how to counterfeit his art.
Obsession sent so swiftly and by secret
A delayed reunion, a distant past
I would better chase an asteroid
Then something moving like her, super-fast.
Branden Rennie hold strong on this course
Put your name on the stars by rights or by force.

If the boys are called and the date is set
A bachelor a wedding and toy plastic guns
If you want an adventure I'll take you
There never was a guy who was more fun.
I'm only a Catholic boy born in June
And she can command a loud symphony
It's just a little early in the afternoon
Is there anyone out there with any sympathy?
So sing delight and conquer night
Bring your guitar to the brook
I swear if you ever show up here
I'll re coop for you however long it took.
Adventure with me: you play, I'll grift
Let's close this rift between you, me, and
Shakespeare.

That she threw up when our courtship began
Let me know I am a find and someone's loss
That she nestled in and never ran
I knew she's less without me, she's imprinted, I'm embossed.
Her femininity in fullest flourish
Adults brought the kids, the young girls cried
Audiences cheered and clapped and blushed
When she sang I sang along, I tried.
I loosed disease at her passion, she returned affection
And since in messages and words and fonts
We have both grasped in each other's direction.
I never broke faith or launched another taunt.
That my love was flat ground and hers high seas
Shows me my heart's as green as summer trees.

I read he left but no I don't know why
Paired with an angel like you, so high
I often look straight to the stars
Asking them pity, tell me where you are.
If at the planet's quarter clock
Or just a side walk through my block
Could bring us closer, I wish you knew
The reason for my life is you.
That he could force himself away
From your sublime attracting gravity
I couldn't want it for myself
I'd rather spin and spinning see
That day by day and night by night
You my love do fine and right.

If you were two while I stayed one
I'd imagine thralls of fun
That far surpasses the ordinary
And pursue lust like a rude fairy.
If heaven sends, then wrong the saints
Devouring you from crown to taint.
Would two be too much past me?
Let's take it to the test and see.
But if you increase your bed past two
But don't host me to pleasure you
I'll fit and bitch and mumble bum
Stranding me alone, just one.
When you arrange your bedroom litter
Leave me out, you'll make me bitter.

When will the woman that I want be mine
And what might I want, it's been so long
I've confused craving with just time
And forgotten only craving is wrong?
How little love I've learned will satiate me
When you do not provide it how I weep
To the refuge of my heart you have the key
Until you come to it, an empty keep.
A storm of tests, songs, promises and delights
Alight vistas of this year's memories
A lacuna of two weeks gave me this fright
Nothing I could do would make you crave me.
I risk assuming to you love's recreation
Say "it's not" ease my appetitive dilations.

Joel you good, you're always making mistakes
Wrongly baiting and dizzying your date
Taking advantage and showing her the breaks
Do you think if you want something it could wait?
I'm young Jeremiah and I have done it all
I have measured tranquility and hurt
I have hurdled thirty years with naught
I'm the one who wishes you would fall.
You're the one who has the truth in knots!
So stop what you're doing and listen to my warning:
That girl you know, tend to her, pamper, sooth
And what you cannot do I'll pick up for you.
Joel you silly dreamer don't let me down
Walk slow and keep your nose to the ground.

Joel you dreamer, now don't run away
Heaven, madness, magic, sin: categories (say)
Of what she can do to blow me away.
I wouldn't have it any other way.
But none are mine and none are your I hope
I'm strung along, hope I'm spared the rope a dope
Wisdom making shapes in every corner
And she's the one parametering the borders.
How she says shoo to other boys than us
Don't make your business or make a fuss.
That I tread my all fours don't count as shoo
And what I say to her goes twice for you.
Joel how I envy magic in your life
Between us I hope you might diffuse the strife.

When music's rythm comes to a curve
And I hear the sound of your lungs intake
Mirroring hearing my body's balance swerves
The tension in your song makes my heart break.
The truth of lyrics sometimes sold and bought
And music videos perchance misread
Makes out if you an icon overwrought
Obscures the feeling under what you've said.
I play the record loud to hear you breath
Wondering if, by listening multiplied
You spiritual life (more life achieved)
If this is true I think you'll never die.
Imagining love that far exceeds creation
I need only your breath as inspiration.

It wets my eyes and makes my heart a stove
I'm so lovesick it hurts me in my chest
If there's pity that touches on your love
You'd give some sign you love me best.
I think if justice, god, were meted right
You are suffering only as much as me
Why do I doubt that fate is bound that tight?
Because you don't appear for me to see.
Taylor, Selby, Judith, Juliet
I'll juggle names if that's what makes you proud
Don't be reckless with what's in these billets
Let the pain that runs through each astound.
The less you give the more I hurt no doubt
By no means let that excuse any shout.

I miss you honey, I feel incomplete Hun
Without you there's a gap hole in my chest
The gravity of a solar ray gun sun
Shoots falling, rushing, wheezing breath.
How could they not discover out heart to heart?
When you talked with me all summer
Gave me my confidence and my start
Did someone imagine I would go under?
I filled with sunshine and blooming smiled
Exploded in my heart (yes that's correct)
Content that autumn to work at raking leaves
My mantle blue, the beads on my wrist red.
I guess new album before next red leaves fall
I think cause there's no stopping you at all.

Disconnect the dots of what she's said
Geometry of half truths, like, what's the problem?
Constellations tumbling through our heads
Blackness of the night sky, the earth revolving
And I love her so I don't go into it
Stars, connections, copper colored heart
She says she wants me, I believe and won't quit
When will this thing that she has planned out start?
Navigation by the lights she's mapped
Is easy for a system wired like mine
In any case a feather in my cap
To read her dreams in letters and in lines
The dot to dot of phantom figures proof
She loves me back and that's enough.

Have you lately imagined her lonely
Gazing at moon soaked skies by herself?
It used to be easy imagining her only
By songs suggesting adventures of stealth.
Is it true she's in constant company?
(How hypocritical of me to think)
If I got her address is never leave,
I'd handcuff myself to the sink.
This era's explosion of sound waves
The stadium of sparkling wrists
If I imagined it would I be delusional
She should be by herself missing my kiss?
That she shines, sings, exhibits and struts
Is she saved from how loneliness cuts?

Can I better express how my eye delights
In her enactment of romantic flights
And how better to prove I am her lights
Then to ask her to love me best. And if
I crumpled up and couldn't breath anymore
With doctors and reverends around me
Would she arrive belatedly with a flower garland,
Hopefully to avoid getting scolded by daddy?
And I'm trying to let you know it's not my fault
If she loves me best (so love me best)
Find out if I'm to blame; she'd be owed by
Venus if I collapsed: a storm of lightening
As if gifts in reply. Would it come through at that point
If she never relapsed into love of call and reply.

You could see right through me and I'll let you
I'll stand a a lectern teaching math by
transparencies.
I'll turn into a hologram for you
Anything you ever wanted to ask to see.
I'd pull it together however I could
So if you don't try to begin seeing me this way
If you want you could lend me your graces
Help me make the promise of my face pay.
And my friends and I are God's heroes
Just for worshiping the Christ mas on Sunday
We were just going to settle the bill with zeroes
But we're on board if your plan is sincerity.
Sweetie let me in, I just wanted
To make it honest, sweetie let me in.

Is there a kingdom and is there a castle?
And would it be hard to scale the wall?
Does it taste like poison, do you want an apple?
Is there any way to rule these people at all?
So we're going to talk about trumps
We're going to race from here to there.
This time we can't be tolerating bumps
If we're going to repair this world of despair.
Can I carry you home, can I lift the disgrace?
Can I make the news any better?
Can I wipe the frown off your face?
It's getting cold come borrow my sweater.
Come see the proof I'm little boy blue
Come see that I'm still in love with you.

Let me say a word about vampires
I hear they got a party in New Orleans.
Where's your sense of adventure (empire)?
Where's your sense of still being Seventeen?
They'll do what it takes to stay forever
You can't tell them they haven't grown up
If they can do it with Reiki and sing-alongs
What's there the devil's going to corrupt?
Our beautiful daughters think it's sunset
Who will you choose to be sever against?
They think they'll see the angels beset
Every one of the devil's encampments.
So many possibilities, give them glamour
So much it hits the eyes like a hammer.

It's a fact that every mortal's dying.
Let's design our tombstones while we're still young.
It's a game of rescues let's start crying.
We can be laughing by the time we're done.
And if my hear got smashed, if it got broken
In fact it didn't, you caught me in the fall
So safe and sound I'll stand by you till the end
Looks like we didn't need good luck at all.
It's a chariot it's on fire it's careering.
It's not limelight you look solid gold to me.
Take back your song we must stop fearing
That I'll leave, I won't, I want to stay and see.
This interdimensional love we've found
Is way too fast to run into the ground.

I could learn everything about everything
And if I learned everything fast enough
Would you say you're the one that's trying to cling
Take a lie and turn it into something with touch?
The world has made some space for some poets
Time to produce something really first rate
Away from you is like being in hermitage
If you could read my writing that would be great.
They're howling at the moon, you're a high
priestess
I'm working on becoming your hierophant
Use this microwave transmission to bridge the
address
Won't be convinced you have another counselor,
you can't.
What magic are you practicing this fall?
You've got me feeling like a sorcerer that's all.

The telephone lines raised by my daddy
Compared to those I was raised second best
Now your job with the telephone company
Makes me think I'll never get a rest.
Enlightenment and communication
(Vexation!) How was I born to all of it?
And how will I ever get liberation
Holding onto a web someone older knit?
New under the sun, I do not deserve
These gifts timing has prepared for me
Not scared to pilot, I'm scared to swerve.
(Athena, Arachne, Penelope!)
To Jason or Ulysses these things would be new
Let's imagine I won't loose too many  crew.

If you leave will I turn to magic circles?
I said I love you unconditionally
Seeking reciprocation has got me purple
I'm just an axle on this fortunes wheel.
You be the unicorn, I'll be the green man
We're both bleeding romance from our veins (our names).
Correspondences of a magic cosmic plan
But the torchlight of your following puts the night to shame.
Can I restore your faith in a little starlight?
In the sky above my neighborhood it's beautiful
Indeed I walk Tailor street every night
The oversight of that has me feeling a fool.
There's so much magic already present
More than passionate I can make this pleasant.

You said you already mothered some children
How enthusiastic I am to hear you fib
Netzach! What a foundation what recompense
Mercy beauty morning sickness baby bibs!
Going dizzy tugging dislodging the gift
Shoulder a rainbow and set off running
I should make some money, buy a car to fit.
Your expectations have got me coming.
My trepidation, and my dancing spasms
The only thing I picture in my dreams
Is your whole world giving you orgasms
Would be enough to make your baby scream
Enough I know just exactly what you mean.
I know I'm moving slowly towards pleasing.
For Malkuth sake tell me you aren't teasing.

How will I see you, you keep me in the dark
Five days I have you and then two days apart
You wouldn't know how Saturday breaks my heart
Will I manage to make a fire by this spark?
I've got this notion about eligibility
It comes from eighteenth century philosophy
When the dictionary, in an infancy
Said there's nothing as accurate as beauty.
No way once you said it I could resist you
You said "New Romantics' now I'm awake
I needed you to know how much I missed you
How a decade wouldn't be too long to wait.
You were twenty five this year that's a quarter buck
I just want honesty about if you'll give me a fuck.

Did you want Temperance and held breath?
Did you want an intellectual ox?
Did you want me to have my fist kiss all left?
Did you want a Catholic who doesn't miss the mass?
It's yours it's safe it's a secret path
To a time when memory didn't cloud love
Should I keep it secret and never ask
Should I always say it's yours and it's not mine?
Ethical theories and ways to perform them
Torture and laughter and making me wait
Every minute is a grating worry
You're never coming back to me for that slice of
cake.
I've got a short list: Leah and Rachel.
But for now I'm wrestling with an angel.

I want to live in a tower, be a prince
I'll ride in on my steed a magic frog
I want to see the jesters make you wince
I want to be your stars that pierce the fog.
Would you take health from me in sickness
Learning medicine strange and effective
Hands off your multi million dollar business
Make some extra money as a private detective.
When I asked you to marry me, I didn't stutter
I thought your reply was very trite
Did you tell that to your mother
Do you regret saying no that night?
Show me what I'm missing, let it all collapse
Fill the empty seat that I've got in my lap.

Imagine the limestone foundations there
Imagine them shaping it physically
Binah and Adonai, the cosmos unawares
Them doing it dirty: crystals and trees.
Making the world out of dust lust and ironies
Let's plant a garden to, let's buy a dog
Name him Adam and teach him to speak
And I'll be jealous of him I won't get along.
You reap the bounty, I'll keep the books
(I know it's just too much to have found each other
This is stupid let's forget how bad it looks
We'll never live it down with your brother).
Generations have generated this
Flood the world with the wet of a kiss.

Like another notch in my belt in reverse.
Illusion that what you presented me with.
Giving you an out I guess I'll regret.
Now you're the empress the world's yours to stir.
I'm still trying to get answered do you want me there?
But I'm a magician, I've got a plan
I'll be an obstetrician, I'll be right there.
Goodness gracious now I'm becoming a man.
You can keep me happy, I'll keep you pampered
And when we're thirty five and in bliss
I'll never think of all that what didn't matter.
Remembering the riddle of when we would next kiss.
Let's start the protests, let's plan the truce
Between the drone bees and the girl spruce.


I've said some things about judgement day (soon)
I've said some things about a deck of trumps.
If I wasn't so sure about saving things from doom
Maybe I wouldn't even like taking my bumps
I've said somethings about loving and sex
I've said something maybe I shouldn't have
I just want to know what's coming next
Am I dreaming? Babe pinch me like a crab!
Only another gift to make you forget
About the structures that bind you, media, and obscenities,
that I'm still addicted to cigarettes,
Morning wood, and the way you talk to me.
These poems might be a little off topic
But in 2022 it's something for your pocket.

"two sonnets apart for little starlight"

I am enraptured by your many riches
I envy your employment true and surely
How did you get awarded these windows
How do you keep the menu so burly?
How would you like to smoke a blunt Little Starlight?
And is it okay if we use this restaurants lawn?
I know it's not legalized in this country yet, but it might.
Why is there so many cars relying on your little brawn?
This fast food paradise restaurant
This midnight method of staying rich
I would be remiss if i lied i can't
You make me look like quite the silly bitch.
The coupons for this place came in the mail today.
Forgive me if i want to see you ever other day anyway.

Little Starlight now that you've come for the smoke
It's time we're all getting herbally cured
Over here where it's polite to hide
There's no Sherlock Holmes detective types to incur.
We're just walking in some alleys we know at night
When no businesses around and no kids.
With a pizza smile and two tea shops providing the light
It isn't vagrancy if i say that it's my youth's thrill.
What is there to be afraid of here in Markham
Please puff puff puff puff and pass the dutchie
Piloting forwards with a warriors' laugh
And no one's worried about getting the munchies.
Little Starlight this good time is all for you.
When they asked how many times you turned me down
you can say: a few.

My wish my sweet, is nothing short of life
And if I say I want you just for you
And if I beg you come be my wife
If you don't want that know this much is true:
If you come and give me my first kiss
Take me to a bed where I'll ravish you
My intention's not pleasure of a tryst
It's the labor that makes three lives out of two.
If you set aside forty weeks to kiss
Ruthlessly, I would take it all for me
Not just a way to catch up for lost time
I want you and me to plant a family tree.
Lie with me in bed for nine months now?
We'll have each other forever anyhow.

Your boyfriend's heart is nothing like the snow
Not ice cold blinding blustery wintry rains
That as soon as it's come down wet it goes
Down the storm drain all clearing and cleaning and
stained.
That's not to say that there's no holes in it.
His heart has cracks and where there's cracks
there's ice
Not to conceit the muscle pump will split
Rather the bearer has seen some sorrows twice.
A few mistakes with cigarettes and pot
A bad record from driving his father's car
A mother who, teaching, can't be taught
A city where the roads span distances: far.
But to insist the rhyme you might demure
Your boyfriend's heart and snow are light and pure.

When I'm deep in the action of waking
Arranging limbs away from under me
Blood won't flow back into my bones until
The phone is quaking and I fall onto the floor
Conjuring me up and now I'm vertical
Or I'm in sunshine and my eyes are open
With your face in the reticle, isn't it?
Why aren't you saying anything congruent?
Well, what would it be worth for making
Waiting into something I waited for?
It's cold outside, it's snow white
I can't wake up from feeling spite.
I'm falling down instead of getting up
Putting a frown up against a ceramic coffee cup.

Darling your legs are the envy of the world
Because of all the places they've taken you
When you get tired you must let the curl
Around something as magnetic and true
The whole quadricep poised, robust and strong
Is necessary for the dance you shake
Babe, you'll dance the streets with me along
I'm a fun guy, you want to maybe date?
Completely stable lightning flashing legs
I've seen them pivot, it's definitely true
That when you spin the question sort of begs
What does the spinning, the whole world or you?
What brings those legs to rest and curl and lie
Should promise you his axis till he dies.

I bet you haven't heard, she's a kinky nymph
I can tell you precisely what she wants
Control the way the mixer spikes the synth
And me! A novice sexual debutant.
One time she did this sexy little bounce
She knew I was looking right at her bum
Now if I reply: "less than an ounce."
She tells me I didn't really even cum.
Over text she prompts me to strip naked
Turn on my camera and stroke myself, exposed
Already, I said, I won't be forsaken
It looks like now I'm taking off my clothes.
There's one thing that I know kept her in love
The way I pressed hard in our parting hug.

The bible's a book I'm just reading in full
But I do know the stories well enough
To tell you that the God whose line I pull
Has definitions of love that come off tough.
At first law and power was his purvey
Explained: vineyardist, pruning at his grapes
Then having caused Job's wretched dismay
Renders the juice and slakes the thirst of hate.
If you believe in synchronicity
If serendipity has caused surprise
Please discuss the holy tome with me
Today I read, tomorrow I'll be wise.
I think this God's our author even now
Transforming: 'swift', from adjective to noun.

What if I am uncomfortable without you?
What if I have a shifting weird disease
That somewhere far away you think I doubt you
Or that, in time, I will fail to please.
I don't want to break up whatever the case
I'm broke and foreign and sleek and fat and young
I still live in a room at my parent's place
Save face and leave me now? Now that's no fun.
At least if you will go shout out the facts
That I was nice to you and very fair
That no matter how crazy you would act
We danced the game like Rogers and Astaire.
I'm really having trouble with my feelings
I just want you to tell me you aren't leaving.

What will you do with all these songs I wrote
The number of them multiplied within
The fraction of the rhymes expressing dote
Cooling the worry of each want and whim?
Hoard them on the website all to yourself
Let them recede into the timeline's fray?
I would want to see them on a store shelf
But you know that I'll do just what you say.
Would you have me, in outrageous deceit
Dedicate them to your alias name
Or plague me with some method of receipt
Tell me my rights were lately signed away?
I'd let you have this one and all the others
If you would like to put me between covers.

When we say 'love' does it become believed?
Before it's heard it's typed then read then thought
I've seen 'love' in all these texts I've received
But an outsider might judge that we're not.
Everything about how this friendship grew
Was at the mercy of how you'd see it pruned
Each time you told me you'd be coming through
I chirped and begged and crowed and smiled and crooned
Well, I guess that it's safe to think you can
Expertly carve the branches and the shoots
With all your fabulous golden acumen
I'll trust you with my heart and with my truths.
The roots of it are deep, the stalk is limber
I hope you plant for shelter not for timber.

Dearest, we have an index without flaws
A paper trail of intrigue, good and bad
But I'm stubborn, my suit, I should withdraw
If I don't get a chance to meet your dad.
Let's calculate the time we've invested
Learning one another's thoughts, cares and quirks
Present the balance for him to contest it
Advise us where the liabilities lurk.
If I were stock and you were a banker
Would you say I was paying dividends?
If I've enchanted your mother, thank her
But if dad says no I think we'd need to end.
Classically we've charted our relations
So, what would be your father's valuation?

You're tired now, and isn't it okay
For you to shut your eyes for just a wink
You're mostly in your bed by early night
Because throughout your day you won't dare blink
From what I can tell, and I can't tell much
You never take reprieve from your routine
In your eyes, I see weariness's touch
You've poured your soul out, that's what I can glean
If you want to survive, to be bolder
You'll shut the blinds and sleep completely stripped
It's too bad you'll wake up just one day older
When you deserve to let much longer slip
You said "I'm tiered" I know just what you meant
Refresh the faculties whose stuff you've spent.

You're here to save me, I want to thank you
You tuck me in at night, I fall asleep
You're here to tempt me, I want to spank you
My affection for you is so complete
Transcendence, lies without dishonesty
A developing psychic dependance
Double dog dare and a rebuke from me
Accomplished without help from the senses.
You got some funny reasons for hiding
You got some interesting things to say
I'm not going to let this thing go sliding
It's set up to bring me higher everyday
Now a tornado couldn't blow me down
Let me know when these forces will bring you
around.

You girl deserve a love letter today
It seems so ling since I wrote you billets
Sincerely I believe you want to stay
Just once to kiss must throb in your regrets.
For months you've kept me batting at the threads
Of a story steeped in disillusionment
With each new catastrophic chapter said:
The more in saying "I love you" I meant
I fully deeply painfully really care
Even if it's a story for my ears
The horror of the sources: yours to bear
And just the relating of it swells my tears
Now you have confided all these terrors
Death take me if to you I fall in error.

Was I arrogant to leave you when I found out?
Was I arrogant to want you in the first place?
Was it shameful for me to not have believed you?
This is your masterpiece of being a rake.
This is me willing to put it all at risk.
This is me willing to try again, despite having failed
I expect that the karma will make you sick.
Every time that you inhale or exhale
I know you're daring and you're ambitious
I know you would pack your belonging up
But I didn't do anything pernicious
I didn't do anything to merit being cucked
This is me forgiving everything to date
This is not having said "I love you" too late.

Did you think you are a rasphode or a courtesan?
In either case it appears you were right
He could be on television all day
You could be on television all night.
A poet, a writer, the first link in the chain
My abundance of caring and desire
Lover you set down roots in my brain.
If this isn't poetry enough set me on fire:
What did you think that would be like
Hitting the target all like Diana?
The sensitive, the hart, the archetype
To the task a total Pollyanna.
Won't you make a sacrifice to me
Knowing in you I see divinity?

Could I embarrass you in front of the guests
Supposing any one of them is reading this
Why don't you let them know you don't have time
To grant me, a friend of yours, his first kiss?
Wasn't I glittering, flattering, and good
Didn't I pull off the mental gymnastics
Demonstrated the appetite, showed you I would
Babe I know you know I think you're fantastic.
This won't be love gone wrong or spiteful
Darling you're the queen of happiness and song
I only want what I wanted: to be delightful
How did our relationship go so wrong?
Kiss me now before this feast of words is finished
Let your guests here know you're not indifferent.

I wish I had been a shepherd hillside
I'd be so unsurpassed at keeping flocks
Maybe then in my love you'd abide
I wouldn't have to make this idle talk.
You could be the shearer and the weaver
I would always flock back to you
I'd be that tailor's greatest believer
If they dyed as colorful as you do.
But it's you who got to shepherd the crowd
You've got only one color to work with blush
So if I hurried to make your face rouge
It was to help you demonstrate the stuff.
Sorry for this brass casuistry
I'm just trying to shepherd you back to me.

I promised you an immovable object
I promised you: you could encompass me
It's been eight years since we touched each other
And I'm still calling you Penelope.
Do you require a change in my orbit?
Do you need me to change the actual sky?
We started so young it would be morbid
For you to ask me why I never asked you why.
Should I posit that this is evolving
As if it's vulnerable to mutation?
I think I'd rather continue revolving
I promised unceasing celebration.
This is a love that functions on it's own
I'm fixed in it, please don't leave me alone.

You did such a fine cameo as a spy
It's doubtless that I fell for your body
There's no persuading you not to lie?
There's no stopping me from talking haughty.
How can he love you the way I love you?
How can it be anything in comparison?
The sacrifices you extracted from me,
I speculate the same would embarrass him.
I've spent my whole twenties trying to please you
I laid siege to your heart and got mistreated
Now with the media telling me otherwise
I'm still not convinced I've been defeated
Perhaps it's better not to have been treated well
Wouldn't deserve heaven if I'd not been through
hell.

Sometimes I wish I had never met you
Sometimes you fooled me until I forgot
A job I worked to afford my shoes
You walked in and tied my heart in knots.
Made friends with the girls I assumed assumed
I know they were too sexy for me to pick up
Had been picked up the moment that they bloomed
That you were blooming just then was my luck
When I figured out I figured out your riddle
I didn't dream you were going to be receptive
But this routine of being second fiddle
Seems to me you think I'm defective.
Was this calculated or improvised
All the sadness you've etched into my eyes?

You gave me lectures on fertility
Quizzed I answered correctly: all of the above
Will there be a test of practical abilities?
Or a thesis course about the root of love?
Has my paper been graded early?
How is employment after matriculation?
If the professor will read it personally?
I'll be fine with a belated graduation.
As an academic I'm persistent,
Is the program running again next semester?
This time could I be your lab assistant?
Of maybe a live tissue sample tester?
If the rhetoric I'm using here is crass
I'm just keen to apply what I learned in class.

What could happen, can you see from this distance
What if they shine the spotlight on me to?
The massive variety of my opinions
Always with conscience shinning through.
Sublunary, I can't tell the night time from the day
Stuck, trapped under this library of mine
I'm never at a loss for things to say,
It's up to you to make things turn out fine.
I'm sure if I was your dancing partner
They'd have no trouble describing our rhyme
Choreographed a little smarter
Keeping time on keeping time on keeping time.
Debating if I love you all the time it's dark,
I answer yes when I hear the morning lark.

You pulled the goddess from me, you used me
You set yourself up against my kingdom
Then you refused me, haven't you abused me,
Is your other boyfriend really so dumb,
He's participating in confusing me?
I have a Christ in me, I have a castle.
Isn't it time that someone scaled the wall?
He's a hermit, he doesn't need the hassle
Why risk bothering his worship at all?
I called you Shelby, I called you sunshine
That wasn't good enough I couldn't bluff you
I stooped to slavery, to calling you divine
Then you stooped to making me so sad
Please pardon me for wanting you so bad.

Hey let's change the subject for an instant
Talk about that supermodel in your crew
It's something that we glossed over isn't it
How if it's your loss then it might be hers' to.
I put you first and I can't take that back
But if you cut me out of the page I'm on
You've cut out a page she's on at that
Maybe she'll retaliate before long
I don't know much about rocket ships
Or about approaching a girl that tall
When she's absolutely on top of the world
I think our break up will look very small.
I want to prepare you for the coming world
I want to ready you for bowing to that girl.

Is there a garden and is there a fountain
And could I have a drink to quench my thirst?
You've had so many lovers let's count them
Could it be beautiful, could you put me first?
All ancient violence stiffing up my thoughts
Homer's Odyssey Homer's Iliad
This skill I paid tuition for, I bought,
Will reading these billets drive you mad?
I have your attention, that's worth a lot
You've got me in detention, you're not talking
You're Queen Juno, you're incredibly hot
I'm throwing lightning bolts, I'm not walking.
A bed of flowers, and a golden cloud
A restless lover and an ancient crown.

I want a leader, I want a modern state
I come to you, I came to harsher rules
I want harmony, I want higher stakes
I forgive you if you're done with these fools.
I want us to be the same and aren't we?
Didn't I rhyme, didn't I make music?
The next time I offer don't depart me
I have no idea why you'd refuse it.
Would we have a party, would we have a wedding
To put faith in me you have faith in me
It's the only way I'd be forgetting
The way you're currently erasing me.
This is me with my hand on the Bible
This is you being adored without rival.

How can you be so glib about your hands?
Those, I have waited long to once more hold.
A siege of years, a starving steady man
Asking you to concede what others stole.
If chat was pulse, I'd know each thump and beat
If your pictures were jewels, I'd choose your rings.
To feel your fingers, cross in mine, to meet,
How empty it all seems without that thing.
Shall I say that your hands are like success:
Deft, strong and un-compared for what they grasp.
Maybe I like them more, you like them less?
Maybe you hate them until they've got mine
clasped.
To holding hands there is no synonym.
I blush about your most sensitive limbs.

How much like the moon I see I am.
Cycling through all and nothing, I appear.
How much like an astronaut you'll be:
Bringing a flag where sands are virgin clear.
For you I must seem something like the moon:
Distant force and fading from bright to black.
Facing you, tranquil, countless mapped out wounds.
My behind matches, but you'll never see my back.
Haven't I done better than extremes?
Questing after, patterns, stories, middles?
Quietly more than simply 'is' or 'seems'
My love for you a backwards facing riddle.
Touch down on me, put kisses on my face
I've orbited you with moon matching grace.

The apostles, transformed on Pentecost
Frightened, called the fire a holy ghost.
Today much of the servant Kings are lost
What is kept, precisely: words they boast.
The business of a haunting ghost, deceased
Is all like Hamlet's father, doom bespoke
Except the heart of Jesus never ceases
Yet, disappeared, this holy ghost evoked.
If we'll suffer this while we're still young:
Out flesh so separate, nothing there to hold,
Then let me put the fire in your tongue
My ghost making your words poltergeist bold.
Holy beauty, holy voice, holy mind
Sharing this with Apostles is divine.

The way a rose blooms, summer, in full sun
Will vex you with six feet or more of thorns
Hired gardeners liable to damage sums
At pruning time, if petaled heads are torn.
Yet if your love's a rose (a good conceit-
It has more thorns than clipped and sold you'd
guess)
I'd love the Garden Rose in its dirt seat
And Wade into the thorns to prune it best.
Am I a garden rose inside your heart?
Towering above the shrubbery of 'friends'
Tendrils shooting creeping thorny growth
With blossoms blushing red up at their ends.
Call me your garden rose and brave the thorns
Tend to me so my bloom exceeds the horns.

Let's hunt the world for soft and soothing rooms
Rent them shortly, put them in our eyes
Curl up under ornamental gloom
As if we are French Monarchs in their prime.
The portals past your skin into your brain
Have been arrayed and overfilled with light
I don't even aspire to make them tame
I haven't got the skill, try though I might.
I think you have been something like a wolf
Now calculating each touch grip and lick
But if we end up something like aloof
Don't worry, know each glance at me will stick.
The circle cast by eyesight, so sincere
Is the only thing we lack between us dear.

Darling, there's no rival to your neck
From photography's start until today
Your eyes and tits got me up on deck
But it's your neck that makes me dig and pay.
I guess I sound like some creepy vampire
Obsessing over where your blood is strong
You're the one that towers like a spire
I'd love to have you for centuries long.
I'd love for you to let me in your mouth
My name, for now, maybe later my tongue
Let me search right down into your neck
Like a giraffe mouth reaching for tree-gum.
I hope this poem gives your heart a lift
Hold it, click! Photograph your neck stiff.

How easily a man like me forgives
I keep karma at bay by staying still
Tears as thick as sweat is what I live
I wipe my face and let myself just chill.
What if I said there's angels in the sky
Exhaling fire and sleet just like in psalms
You think I want revenge? I will not lie:
I simply pray and God will right the wrong.
If you had suffered half as many wounds
To your heart as I have, let's compare
You'd take your money, spend it on the doom
Catch the cheats dead sometime they're unaware.
Seething like King David in the Bible
As much as I love you I hate my rival.

If all the witchcraft in the world can work
How doomed the whole rest of the world is
I trace the stencil of the circle unsure
Just how much of a shit the demons give.
I have prayed for all of the superpowers
In days gone by the priests themselves would tote
Meet me at in the chamber of my magic tower
We'll command a roaring flood to fill the moat.
Look into the grimoires to find out
Just what the secret whims of mankind are:
To stay in bed and rule the world from dreams
With oil pastels and wishes to various stars.
I can't foresee the effects that I'll cause
Sadly though, I don't know how to pause.

Faust my man, did you see me come through
And save your wretched Gretchen from the jail
Where she might die so that you could pursue
Hellen, as if some Maori hunting whales.
There's nothing wrong with Gretchen I insist
Her thirst for jewels just makes her more sincere
How glad I am you left her in the mist
I'll take your greedy girl and call her dear.
Imagine I am something like a rogue
Not a mage all banner-ed with diplomas
I steal what I like and I like your ex girl
While you stand at your tripod huffing soma.
You tricky beast Mephistopheles
Take Faust to feast while Gretchen and I leave.

I guess you thought that I had writer's block
My pen's been stubborn for a year or two
Actually what happened was not so stock
You hated the first series, and I withdrew.
Tell me is there a pen that gets griped tighter
Then mine when I am at my empty page?
A B A B G G so says the fighter
I'm spilling the ink now, observe me rage.
Don't you think writing's a lot like sex?
Commanding the line to stay taught and springy
I've been so confused, sure I've been vexed
But mostly, unconsented, I've stayed stingy.
Now you'll take my style all rough draft
Let's see if this time you admire the craft.

When finally the sun gets out of sight
I breath sweet relief and think of you
To process all the brightness of the day
Just distracts from a better view.
You know our brains are just like a modem
Dealing with data in and data out
The sun and clouds must surely overload them
And woman's figure a protocol that routes
The hunger in the gut, the swollen sin
The pacing of the day and remembering death
The hottest sunlight ushering sweat from skin
Execution of these programs: woman's behest.
Finally when we power down our eyelids.
Set your screensaver to dream of us as kids.

I saw you fried your hair you showy girl
And all the strands are wavy with over use
You'd be mistaken if you think I care
And I would never take it as option to abuse.
Your hay-gold pretty locks are frayed with style
It's fine, I know that's part of the big show
Let me tame it, it's chastened but still wild
Its not like fried hair doesn't feel wind blow.
The blonde of a girl who was seven years old
Pale gold blond from pictures your mom shared
Will over throw all outrage in my soul
Will same wise fry the basis for my fear.
Come to me and let me comb you waves
My arms are safe you need not be so brave.

Sex mania? Not really. No. You charmed me.
That's not to say I am not inclined
Let's say that you took me out in public
And I saw you kissing cheeks: nope that's no longer fine;
You ask if I am horny while my mind
Is whirling with just poems to confuse you
But let's say I see you begin to stray?
Yeah, I'll take that as signal to make use of you.
Now I know the secret down to facts
I saw some scans of the inside of sex
A brain totally reeling with distress
While all the male senses are retained.
Don't outrage my love now I must insist
And if you do I'll insist with my prick.

You dare to keep me waiting for a year
This time I had no hope of you returning
Meanwhile our friend (the tall one, you know who)
Has been collecting every penny I've been earning.
I am a soldier's son and you forgot
My uncle's have day labored all their life
Now you are back and now you ought
To stay put, guess what, now I'm in the light.
I have a little cadre of good fans
All the ones a man like me could wish
Older eyes, a literate elite stans
And they know every beat of our dish.
No underestimating me this time
The stakes are high and we're a perfect rhyme.

I am a better angel than you prayed for
I am the soft and pliant kind of flier
in unquenched hope I save your soul I muster
another round of verses for this sad mire
if there is violence in the body you walk as
i will have no piece of body then I assure
If the multitude you entertain lacks manners
I will tilt the scales of manners by love pure
forgiveness and soul saving is not naturally
the plight of pedestrian man very often
but with this train of time behind humanity
sometimes what's insisted is really a prophet
Like frantic Jonnah preaching in Nineveh
I'll blot out all the smears on your soul's day.

The strategy of chat, this hazy risk
Where what you say and who you are all play
Tractors me in for endless hit and miss
I'm tilting at windmills all night and all day.
It's a fantasy I had: everyone clear cut
Just who they were exactly who they must be
The way it is? A veil over everyone
Some eggshell white, others: embroidery.
I hope you see me in the chat right now
My homemade bios like Quixote's helm
Strike one? Oh no this is where I shut down
Cause strike out and get banned would just be hell.
Banter swift as lightening marveling all
If you need someone witty at me y'all.

At some point I got cold about this thing
This thing they tell you when you're young: make friends
Never came to me real easily
So I got technical in regards them.
Have you ever helped me with my aims?
Or sat with me like I was just like you?
Have you got something nurturing for my brain?
Sorry then we're not a pair, we're two.
"You're simply not invited to the castle."
"My heart's a private kingdom" you announce.
Well that's fine and I'm no serf, spare me the hassle
You got no plans to have fun so I'll bounce.
Yet I would melt back into that childhood trance
If you took me to your castle for a dance.

Always I have a man's body at hand
It's mine, I like the flat broad of my chest
How my stomach squares 'round the obliques
Yes also I love my own stalk the best
Then bottom of my rump sits square and full
Okay my feet are weird you got me there
Thighs like hydraulic lift presses curl
Everything topped with crop short brown hair.
Woman goes here and there bragging the same
I have a man's body always at hand
Hands though, being the name of the game
Just how handsy will you be getting ma'am?
Tell me what you'll do with all my flesh
Or else risk let me doing what I like best.

The late spring blossom of Venus-good flowers
had me thinking on my love as a Goddess
something adjacent suddenly paused my mind:
what of those who esteem my love less?
no quicksilver applause for you in chat?
no cross-armed consideration of your soul?
in the cloudy way i whip up fantasy
now I consider the bleak abyss bellow.
Let's make clear how i regard my love:
She is a renaissance queen in my wits-eye
Dancing, singing, costume-playing girl
whose skies are either crystal or storm's eye.
When you regard my love, regard her well
Esteem her surpassing heaven and trouncing hell.

Tonight I pace my porch and face the stars
Address the seven spheres with: woe is me!
I have a glut of same similar nights
Where all my hours stargazing are lonely.
I guess we're like the planets in our way
we have our space and time and mass and swing
but mostly orbit distance all polite
our poems lapping around us just like rings.
Lonely porch will become lonely bed
I'll color in a talisman citing Mars
you'll sing a prayer for mighty Mercury
I'll toss and turn with emptiness in my arms.
A shooting star grabs my skyward face
An outer space kiss setting the sky ablaze.

Wouldn't you know I swallowed fairy tales
From 'Once upon a time...' until "The end."
"happily' pervading the lexical
In devil's perch or princess's thrilling win.
Mostly when I put eyes upon the world
I spare 'wonder' for 'science'; 'end' for 'now'
But when I set my fingers to pencil twirl
I set everything beautifully anyhow.
Can you be old and still brave children's stories?
With "beast" and "kidnap" rollicking through the plot?
These middle-modern myths are never boring,
And adults observe what children just do not.
I'm not a prince but I'll use text to charm
"Dream come true" until you're draped across my arms.

Can't stress enough how tough it is to read
Turning pages, scanning letters 'till I'm tired
some legendary novel in front of me
and my head on the pillow all expired
What need I of books when your love's mine?
The years of romance between us has it's magic
those disparate moments of being in reach in time
Makes novels on the topic all seem ratchet.
All this is true yet these things grind me worse
Than deciphering the prose of novel books
I barely have your point of view, my love
Could you clarify this, is it as dire as it looks?
That life has published romance on our souls
Makes me wish you'd set your hand to prose.

It's late spring now and you must be compared
To refreshing warmth of late May glory days
Blue skies like your eyes, wow I see they're fair,
And breezes sweet as the songs of yours I'll play.
Good thing the planet keeps orbiting on and on
When it's not spring her beauty's uncontested,
Our deer-park secluded story moving on
I'll say that in contest, she's never bested,
Let's bicycle away to some nice glen
And as our feet are dangling in the brook
In the moment where the suns hot and our feet wet
Then I'll kiss you in rivalry to all that is good.
The winter of our loving all in the past
By the brook our hands and lips will meet at last.

A nightmare now, one I had of your suitors
Besting me, outshining me so much
In nightmare they appeared as gambling satyrs
Lighting and then dousing fires to your love.
In that bad dream I appeared behind the satyrs
In the shape of a giant arachnid
Bringing something madder in love than fire
I carried you off wrapped in a web I knit.
Go read on nightmares lovers have of rivals!
Othello or Odysseus to name two
No doubt my bad dream only got more wild
I'd like no more of rivals please, thank you.
That they appeared as satyrs in my dream
I wonder they were all less than they seemed?

"That's my husband bitches" chortles one
Dashing all the dream of the renaissance
so, if that's the way it's going to be
let's give your bitch-pack friends something they
want.
the emails between us are completely sex
it carried on behind the other guys back.
If we're married I didn't get the text
the doctor signed me over? tell them that!
I bet you bragged that I don't use your name
you tell me what you want and I agree
You prank and I'm down for it all the same
Marry me without my knowledge, probably!
Explain your exuberance instead of testing
I won't stall, I'm your very best thing.

Tonight my soul is soaring, I discerned
So I took my pen and set it to my page.
By your disarming visit here's what you earned:
My soul found peace, you quelled it of rage.
Perhaps you are less assured right now
I wouldn't reach you, I withheld my hand.
But oh! If eyes can touch then you're devoured;
I gazed at you with all my heart's demands.
And you with your five fingers in a claw
Reached riskingly to stroke my marred tattoo
Took all my love you knew was housed in straw
And promised it was vaulted, treasured, true.
Inspiration often fails me, sorry babe
When I do grasp it "I love you" is what I say.

Where are your friends I asked, and you said: me
And in a moment's honesty decoded
The horror of the marriage at your back
What fame has done to friendships all eroded.
Well lucky me to want the woman whole
To all her needs and dreams I have surrendered
Each week I pay alms at my goddess' bowl
No ransom but true love will I have tendered.
Where are your friends, who helps you with your aims
They're lofty good and smart beyond compare
The rolls are empty? Nothing lost, nothing gained?
Get me beside you and we'll reclaim your share.
Education failed them all to not explain
A friend's another self in health or pain.

Ethics in Short

People have a hard time just saying that apples are good and murder is bad, but I wouldn't want a bruised apple in my salad of a dead body in my house. Since sometimes bruised apples and dead bodies show up one way or another, it's good to keep some whiskey around; but only under lock and key.


Apples are good and murder is bad
And Joan-on-the-bones is confusing your dad.
Three thousand years, I can't recall much
Neither can Joan is all seems a rush
Sokrates is wrong and Plato is mean
Let's start with the beginning so Joan don't scream.
Cynics are gross they jerk off outside
First thing Joan knew when she opened her eyes
Two-thousand-one porno internet
No wonder that girl bought a hunting net.
Did it again three steps forward two back
Epicurus got buried in Socrates dull attack
Jesus set you all straight but Jerusalem crumbled
Joan-on-the-bones doesn't need to not mumble.
In the new church we argued about will
Omniscience, omnipotence, oh what good thrills!
Joan-on-the-bones becomes omnipresent
When she opened her textbook
And it simply said this: If you can't get laid
That's something bizarre
Monkeys can do it, why aren't you hard?
Let's cut the shit like Occam with a razor,

Time travel is bunk go holler at the stargazers.
Enter Old Nick: "Well, love, hate or fear?"
Who cares just like Joan we're thirsty come here.
It's only a crime if you're caught we agreed
Your mom's at the movies got the tickets for free.
Here's what we know, it's real tough to lie
You can only brag about something you tried.
Russell tried condensing ethics so we could read quick
But that didn't do it so Oxford's back thick
Irwin: two thousand six hundred pages I smothered
And Joan-on-the-bones isn't your mother.
What's best for the most is most for the best
That's not controversial, give it a rest.
If it's sticky it sticks, if it's wet it slides
I'm not being glib Puefendorf's my guy.
No one becomes happy in little pieces
Ask the Queen or God or Leibniz (to be descent).
But don't ask your dad, he's busy with money
And as happy as he is now, don't get funny.
Hume is a dunce, I'm not going to cry
No Hume no Dennett, and I hate that guy,
Rousseau is no better and word is he was crazy
Well no shit what happened his publisher's lazy!
To print that thin book and call it ethics to boot
Was the most heinous crime of 1762
Notice I didn't say boo about Butler
I'm on call for Joan and board so let's rhyme more
About ethics through time
And what's right and what's wrong
Until I'm at your dad's backdoor
With a carpet and tongs.

Kant's just like me we both like our walks
Through provincial towns with municipal clocks
What he meant by is / ought it's not hard to grasp
But I doubt that your dad was up to the task.
No Hegel no Marx, no Marx no Stalin
So utilitarianism goes into the bin?
What's best for the most is most for the best
That's not controversial, give it a rest.
Schopenhauer has a four syllable name,
He's delusional bad and wrong for the game
Kierkegaard is better but that's where I'm lost
Aesthetic and virtue? I preferred Kant's clocks.
It's just after midnight mom's still not here
Will there be gunshots? Will I smell fear?
Beyond good and evil's a nice name for a spine
From my spy-monitor I see Joan's behind.
Mill tries so hard, so does Sidgwick, Green, Ross
To keep utilitarianism from loss
But over the mountains and under the sea
Authoritarians will not let it be.
So say what you will and do what you want
Maybe it's all thrills maybe it's sum art
Me I'm just fine with what Joan wants
Right now that's to hoist this carpet to a haunt
Won't say what he did or why he's on the pyre
I follow orders and Joan is tired.
When daybreak comes through
And the atmosphere chills
You look out at the sky say the sunrise looks ill
Joan and I cash our cheques and go home
Maybe sometime soon your mom will to.
That's all there is I won't say it three times

So prick up your ears and remember the line:
Apples are good
And murder is bad
And Joan-on-the-bones
Is confusing your dad.

Branden Floydrennie, MMXXII

Lightning Source UK Ltd.
Milton Keynes UK
UKHW022142090223
416682UK00016B/2354